Skirmish

Also by Dobby Gibson

Polar

Skirmish

Poems

Dobby Gibson

Graywolf Press
SAINT PAUL, MINNESOTA

Publication of this volume is made possible in part by a grant provided by the Minnesota State Arts Board, through an appropriation by the Minnesota State Legislature; a grant from the Wells Fargo Foundation Minnesota; and a grant from the National Endowment for the Arts, which believes that a great nation deserves great art. Significant support has also been provided by the Bush Foundation; Target; the McKnight Foundation; and other generous contributions from foundations, corporations, and individuals. To these organizations and individuals we offer our heartfelt thanks.

Published by Graywolf Press
2402 University Avenue, Suite 203
Saint Paul, Minnesota 55114
All rights reserved.

www.graywolfpress.org

Published in the United States of America

ISBN 978-1-55597-515-9

2 4 6 8 9 7 5 3 1
First Graywolf Printing, 2009

Library of Congress Control Number: 2008935596

Cover design: Kapo Ng@A-Men Project

Contents

2

For Scarlett Moon,
who is my greatest fortune

A poem is written by someone not the poet
to someone who is not the reader.
Paul Valéry

 When you count the villagers,
you have to count the scarecrow.
Ko Un

Refuge

Every story gets old beginning
the moment it begins being told.
I'm "more here" with each such moment.
My agent is disbelief.
My story might be real.
I'm not bleeding, but full of blood, I have potential.
My story has no pages,
just its own, ancient chemistry.
What are you waiting for?
We will never be summoned.
Close your eyes and let's practice
what comes next.
We have to escape while we can.
I'm trying to remember you—quick,
now you try to remember me.

1

Mercy

My latest wish to take it all back
now lies in state
in the fluorescent light of the rotunda,
beneath just a fleeting notion of escape,
like the thought of running up the down
escalator in the shopping mall I never wanted
to go to in the first place.
The morning after the morning after,
there's no turning back.
There's still that switch that switches on nothing,
there's still a light that will never go black.
It's over, says the split wood to the nail.
We're just getting started, says Cruelty,
blowing into town, blasting Sabbath from his van.
All at once where I live
and seemingly everywhere I don't,
hissing why at the sky, my God,
I've done terrible things.
The band plays on.
Crows scream in congress.
A butcher stands behind glass
and pounds the market's meat.
The universe expands in every direction
simultaneously at the speed of light,
but expands into what?
At the edges, it gets extremely dense.
It's all held together by eye contact.
In the center stands your father,
and in his bowl is just enough batter
for one last pancake.
We are born in tiny collisions.
Buttoned into our best suits
we eventually drift apart.

What It Feels Like to Be This Tall

Not one of my costumes is believable.
I'm constantly away on business.
The morning, chiropractic, saddles me
beneath its colossal gravity.
In search of a breath, kneeling at the shallows,
the minnows scatter.
Wind farms hum atop the prairie.
Wilt Chamberlain's bones groan from their earthen locker.
In my most private thoughts,
radio signals from distant lands
argue invisibly over static,
and like an ice-cream headache,
the only thing worse than feeling this way
is not having a reason to feel this way,
hoping against hope, against nature,
versus self—I miss you all so much. Send money!
I don't have a fight song,
yet isn't that alone reason enough to fight?
Let the academics roll their eyes.
Faced with a progressively larger fork
for every subsequent course,
at some point, even my belongings began to mock me.
I couldn't eat another bite.
I'm starving.
Whatever you love most
is just another thing for me to bonk my head on.
I can't even trust a kite.
Above the rest of you, from the back row
of my second-grade class photo,
Kristin Dahlberg and I could see giraffes migrate the Serengeti.
Our knees ached with empathy.
Their hearts were as big as basketballs.

Tribal drums called us from the distance.
The distance called us from the distance.
Soon, everything would get knocked over,
and yet we would come in peace.

Fortune

Your luck for today:
The desire to have any is your first mistake.
The second, knowing this, is to hope
to be somehow outside of it all,
and this will set in motion an architecture of great consequence.
Rivers will vanish into rivers,
Sunday will bring half-price bottles of wine, cruets edged with light.
How many times have you walked at night,
sheaves of gloom precluding a neighborhood
singing in its own intense, quotidian silence?
A single dog will bark.
You will get your wish, but it may arrive too late.

Fortune

We think we are little gods,
yet the one thing we fear most is to be left alone.
So we carve one another's names into the desktops,
drop rocks from the trestle.
We invent and overuse the long vowel.
To be loved, speak with your hands.
To learn how, open a magazine
and try to catch the little cards as they flutter to the floor.
Some numbers come with secret powers.
Some secret powers come with little power at all.

Why I'm Afraid of Heaven

If you stood on Venus,
where the atmospheric haze
is so thick that it bends light,
it theoretically would be possible
to stare at the back of your own head.
Which would mean you'd never
again have the pleasure
of helping a beautiful woman
fasten the clasp on her necklace.
On Jupiter, a beautiful woman
might weigh 400 pounds,
but so would you,
and you'd be far more worried
about suffocating to death
on planetary gas.
We've all desired what we can't find here.
We've all left our gum beneath the seat.
In a bright department store,
a plastic egg gives birth to pantyhose.
In a dark dorm room,
a lonely freshman finally gets his wish.
The dog tries, and fails, to run across the ice.
After spending a lifetime
conscious of being alive,
why would anyone
want to spend an eternity
conscious of being dead?
In this bar, one of the world's last remaining pay phones
hangs heavy in the corner.
Most days it waits in silence.
Once in a while, it just rings and rings.

Are We There Yet?

You only have to make her one grilled cheese
in the suffocating heat of summer
while still wearing your wet swim trunks
to know what it's like to be in love.
And you only have to sit once
for a haircut in the air conditioning
with the lovely stylist to forget all about it,
and to forget that anything in the universe
ever existed prior to the small, pink sweater
now brushing softly against your neck.
In this world, every birth is premature.
How else to explain all of this silence,
all of this screaming,
all of those Christmas card letters
about how well the kids are doing in school?
We're all struggling to say the same old things
in new and different ways.
And so we must praise the new and different ways.
I don't like Christmas.
I miss you that much.
For I, too, have heard the screaming,
and I, too, have tried to let it pass,
and still I've been up half the night
as if I were half this old,
and like you, I hate this kind of poetry
just as much as my life depends upon it.
They're giving away tiny phones for free these days,
but they've only made
a decent conversation more precious.
One medicine stops the swelling,
another medicine stops the first medicine.
Just like you, I entered this world
mad and kicking, and without you,
it's precisely how I intend to go.

Fumage

The truth is often what you at first don't trust,
a day born in the fog, another morning
of a morning wanted over.
Everyone in bad jackets,
stepping out into their lives
of doing the already done, tiny happiness,
a white paper bag full of sweets.
The surrenders are everywhere,
though surrendering isn't what it used to be,
and what it used to be
is what the flags at full mast mourn.
This neighborhood kid discovers matches,
that large suitcase stands packed by the door.
This is a day born in traffic
and here comes its tunnel.
This is the sound of a thousand
radios going _____,
proving once and for all
that the art of having something to say
has become the art of having nothing to say,
but more beautifully.
We fail words.
All flus come from China.
This is a day born with an old friend's wave,
and because you saw it,
there goes your chance,
and because you didn't take it,
this is the mark it leaves in your sky,
one that will never wash away
in the day's noisy time machine,
even as you yield to it
in the countervailing doubt
that has become a faith in its own right.

A janitor flips the switch,
and the whole school falls dark.
A wind blows, and a hundred
umbrellas explode black in the rain.

Fortune

The stylist steams the silk blouse,
dressing her mannequin in silence.
The plot unfolds into mystery.
The couch unfolds into a bed.
You buy gas from a grouch
encased in shatterproof glass.
He has a special slot for the twenties.
The priest stops at the cleaners
to retrieve the robes of his Hallelujah chorus.
He swims in lakes, but he makes sure
to never touch the stuff at the bottom.
You wear expensive shoes,
which you sometimes use to kill spiders.

Chin Music

He sat at the kitchen table, waiting for his wife. He knew she had gone, but he didn't know where. As he sat there he realized, for the first time, their chairs didn't match, but in a way that had always been exactly right. He wondered whether robots thought about such things. He decided they probably would be programmed out.

He was an umpire renowned among his kind for inventing a new and more elaborate gesture indicating that a strike had been thrown. She was a composer suffering from writer's block while trying to pen a fight song for the local school for the deaf.

For years, they had slept back-to-back. They never spoke of it, each sure it meant nothing. She had taught herself to lie by saying that which is most obviously true, but only to obscure all that might not be. He had learned to lie by pretending that she was not doing so in the first place, and in this way they had grown to love one another more deeply.

As he waited, he watched their dog commute the inside of the backyard fence, wearing a path of frustration at the perimeter of its world. The night sky ran black, like the motel sink water a crook had dyed his hair in.

When she finally did walk through the door, she startled him. Her hair and coat were wet, and they sent rivulets of water to the floor. She looked at him for a moment, then laughed and said, "My God, it's really raining."

Truce

Perhaps this can be understood
only by someone who has already had
the thoughts expressed here,
someone who knows
that you can't truly understand a word
until you're already in desperate need of that word,
like *afternoon*,
like sitting in front of an open summer window,
old guitar falling slowly out of tune.
So far, I have learned very little.
I want to, for instance, but can't,
render this in something realer,
in a *leaves* that not only blesses leaves,
but in a *leaves* that makes them more so.
There is a new word for uncertainty,
and an old word for permanence
that was recently forgotten.
But there is no dictionary for this,
there's just that hawk there
circling above the river
to perfectly name the way the clouds
blow past us as impossibly as prepositions.
Of this language, which is sometimes not reassuring.
To whatever happens next, which I deserve.
Whatever I can say.
Whatever great light
or greater reason why.
Whatever song that's better once it's been heard before.
It's a powerful idea
to have had the idea before.
I'm so close to this idea, I'm burning.
You've been holding me back.
You saved my life.

Fortune

Another iceberg calves and drifts
its first few feet toward destruction.
The motel hallway carpeting just goes on and on.
A cigarette is flicked from a speeding car,
a farmer files his horse's teeth—
how is it that we can *ever* fall asleep?
There's an infinity inside even
the shortest storms of our seen lives.
A Finn ladles water over his sauna rocks.
He's never met you, and that is why
he has to make himself feel better
by going someplace very small to be warm and alone.

Fortune

There's only one horizon, yet it can be found
in every direction we look.
You'd think it would be easier to get the hell out of here.
Just ask an iceberg.
In any Chinese restaurant, never order the 42.
Never answer your door during dinner,
it's probably another little shit peddling Snickers.
Posing behind their windows,
the mannequins remind us of their absent stylist.
This is all hero worship.
This poem ends the same way they all do—
list everyone you've ever had sex with here:

July, July

Let us hope we are succeeded
in this world by the beauty
that preceded us.
Yes, I'm staring.
Do you remember me?
I was the one looking up the tracks
for the train, or even
just the headlight of a train,
anything that might offer
another foggy promise of arrival.
From every direction, the city
filled the neighborhood
with its surgical hum.
And then evening began to unload
its freight of infinite darkness,
or whatever spell
you were under that allowed me
to first stand there and watch
you remove your clothes.
I love you so much it's dangerous.
I don't regret a thing.
There are rewards
for which there will be no accounting.
The princess blows gently
across the surface of her apricot tea.
The storm reaches the unsuspecting coast.
Finally breaking free, the pier
is swallowed into the foam.
What boiling point?
Some collisions require no cause.
I fell into the river and, lucky for me,
now you're my wife.

Exit Strategy

As for the day bluely begun,
it's already yet another one
beginning to deliquesce,
not so different, after all,
from last year's paint
still hiding behind the radiator.
There is a silence there so thick
the future can be heard
whispering back to the past.
It says, *Life is best lived shared,*
but only when it can't be lived
completely alone.
Each, after all, is just another form of luxury.
Sparrows line the billboard
advertising the development
that destroyed their previous habitat.
From the inkwells of summer puddles
tires scrawl a cursive across the pavement
that evaporates before we can decode
what it's trying to say.
Unless that *is* what it's trying to say,
that to vanish before rendering meaning
is itself a lasting statement,
like the preservationists
huddled over the Renaissance masterpiece
and swearing their profession's only oath:
everything we do will be reversible.
Even as another tea bag drains
its last, dark thoughts into the sink.
Another swimmer shakes the sea
from her ears.
Another archeologist gasps
as she uncovers the vase fragment

while another coroner discovers
yet another reason why,
and another boy with a balloon
looks into his mother's eyes
and suddenly lets it go.

Ode to Unconventional Beauty

It exists because and not in spite
of the gap between Lauren Hutton's front teeth,
it's comprised partly of its own absence,
it's seeing another peel the orange
so that it all comes off in one piece.
You're full of ideas you can't explain.
You once left your favorite glasses on a train.
A truck backs slowly down the dock,
rain falls on a forgotten lock, hung rusting,
birds on the phone poles,
thinking they're still real trees.
You didn't know what to think of her
until the perfume hung there
long after she left.
All winter, the sun fell through the window
just so, and now, in spring, the old dog
has no idea where to sleep.

Fortune

You are the very stranger your mother warned you never to speak to.
And yet here your life's most rewarding conversation continues.
It comes with old songs you can't shake,
and directions to the homes your friends haven't haunted for decades.
Cartography: who needs it?
You'll know you're separated from the herd
when you hear the neighborhood chant its ancient requiem.
The whole place is bugged.
You may not be able to recollect how you got here,
but you wake up every morning, don't you? So wake up.
Fall asleep on the courthouse steps until a nightstick prods you.

The Battle Hymn of the Republic

The lost explorers and sled dogs still preserved intact
beneath sixty decades of snow know
something about this window's transparent insistence
on framing the crippling distance,
and the distance, so cloudless, so devoid of sea,
runs away from us in every direction like a child.
Here, who could possibly need to "work" on a tan?
Without even the suggestion of a current,
there's a sense of invasion, or always planning one,
days starched into being, planted
like trees to memorialize themselves,
a rusted bike lashed to the fence
like a forgotten *Gunsmoke* pony.
In the truckers' mirrored sunglasses rises
the continental mountainry that obscures the valley
where the shadow was invented.
Emerging from it, it can be argued
whether our best days are behind us or ahead,
though we all agree they aren't here now.
The present has arrived only for repair.
An incomplete set of encyclopedias
stands at attention atop the mantle,
and beyond S-Sn lies the unknown.
It's all so hard to believe. Sometimes we just whistle.
The water tower stands as temple
to our considerable thirst,
something we might climb to swap
a little usefulness for longing, reminisce about later,
and then find some sleep in whatever darkness
lies just beyond the road lights.
Where fathers refuse to talk to their sons.
Where the mothers of the Daughters
of the American Revolution bequeath

their unfinished games of solitaire to the ghosts
now skipping through the orchards in their diaphanous gowns.
The presidential election cycle is the only stopwatch
able to clock how slowly the sleepwalkers shout commands
from the abandoned battlefields now ruined with barns,
everything painted in a red that used to be red,
every clarinet rehearsing an old anthem
about a new silence delivering its unthinkable account,
like that sudden bump in the boulevard
that reminds us of all those bodies in the trunk.
As the storm approaches. As the plains
are danced by their invisible ballerinas of loneliness.
As the bent-hanger antennae quiver atop their staticky Trinitrons.
Old Ironsides heaves with asthmatic regret.
Every way home is the long way home.
Even standing there at your faucet, filling a pot for tea,
you know you will never arrive,
and so fear you have always been born to fight.

2

Since We Last Met

I.

The kitchen window showed nothing but Coming Attractions.
All stories appeared to end in a great darkness.

Soon I realized: they weren't actors,
they were my family.
When the larger ones leaned down to kiss me,
they stank.

There was an old doorbell connected
to nothing. She became my favorite teacher.

Dear Sun and Water,
was this really what you had intended?

It was thought that dogs could smile.
It was also hoped.

II.

Like a seed, a coin was placed in my hand,
and just like that, a great debt was born.

Into the park we carried the zero
where it shattered at dusk,
offering us a final proof: we were loved after all.

The mob didn't know what it had surrounded,
yet this became the reason it grew thicker.

Our problem: we feared everything.
Our strategy: blend in through relentless agreement.

We watched the snow keep its balance atop the fence.

III.

The search party was a smash.
My gibbering associates giggled
every time the phone rang.
Among the altos,
the first chair remained impervious to my solicitations.

If there are feelings,
then there must be a reality that causes them,
but in the space that exists between the two,
our finest lies are born.

The electrical empire expanded
to include larger miracles of convenience
as a great carelessness employed many.

When you're sorry for what you did,
you're usually sorry for what you didn't.

IV.

It was all real, and I would never recover.
The search party whispered,
If only we could start over again.

Eternity wasn't an extension of time,
but the absence of it.
The grid strained to make sense
of its own dimensionlessness.

It felt as if someone was waiting for me,
but where?

When I imagined my death,
I was sure I could make it original.

I wondered: will this kind of death
punish me for my mistakes,
or will I find you there instead?

Fortune

You will find great happiness in an old friend.
You will never find your lost cat.
A single broadcast frequency can hold
1.2 million conversations simultaneously.
Toothpaste, first invented by the Egyptians,
contained sand and caused immense pain.
Your neighbors know more about you
than does your own mother.
That man across the street
who you assume is reading the newspaper isn't.
You have a bright future in computers.

What Was to Be Now Is

Often there is no surer way
than just standing there on your own two feet,
the blizzard on approach,
the crows bending back to the earth, then gone.
Hulls knock secret warnings from the boathouse
as if to let us know it was all coming to this,
the world about to snow itself
right back into one dimension.
But despite what you were once taught,
there's no one listening to these thoughts,
or so you now assure yourself,
suddenly noticing the reflection
in the window there,
like the ghost of a kid brother
who had died at birth
or been held back many, many grades.
Earlier, on the highway,
acetylene flares traced the outline
of a mortal wreckage in orange,
as if hope was now
another charming construct of the past,
not even something we might
pray to glance in passing,
like that new pair of shoes
we were once sure would solve it all.
On the one hand, there are other hands,
and for this we give thanks.
The first door is the one you entered through.
The rest are there only for fires.

Puncture

First they tear off the oldest layer,
but only if they're not hammering on the new
as if the old were never there.
Sometimes they just tear the whole thing down.
Once in a while they walk away
until the rain comes through.
The first known roof, according to experts,
was called a *skull*.
It proved vulnerable in winter and fragile to repair.
So man used grass, which worked fine
until he discovered fire.
There once was a roofer who lived
a full life even though a steel stake
had been driven through his forehead.
Too dangerous to remove, said doctors.
He never forgot a grocery list,
though he thereafter referred to his mother as Ron.
Just give me a good roof over my head
and I'm happy, he was known to say.
The history of brain surgery
can be traced to the discovery
of sharpened obsidian during the Stone Age.
For centuries, the only patients were kings.
The history of successful brain surgery reads more quickly,
though the first step has forever been the same: bad haircut.
Side effects include agraphia,
an inability to write intelligibly
caused by disruption to the parietal lobe
of the dominant cerebral hemisphere,
which blazing chairs unworthy
seem part of no way proving encyclopedias
free of their tobacco smoke.
Thus concludes our visit to the surgical theater.

Outside, one story closer to heaven,
nail guns explode in celebration of repair.
Roofers stir pagan vats of goo,
backs slickened, glowing cancerous in the sun.
A good roof will breathe a little.
It should always be highest in the middle.
To survive the blow, first lean into the impact,
then simply live as if the wound had been there all along.

Fortune

It can never be that way again.
Every neighbor is, to some degree, a spy.
When you arrive, they will have been expecting you.
And still a cold wind washes silver through the gate.
Smut glows from behind the gas station registers.
Most things float when they die.
They need you in wardrobe, fair enough, but who's this "they"?
Consider yourself warned: there's no question
more dangerous than *How have you been?*

Fortune

The neighbors will soon spread their confounding potluck before you.
Dressed in period garb, they wear sandals with socks.
They subscribe to *Life* magazine to experience
the present as if it were already the past.
Their flowering trees were engineered to never drop fruit.
Overhead, constellations of stickers glow from bedroom
ceilings as souvenirs from a time when life was lived outdoors.
All conversations end in silence. The trick is to make it purposeful.
It's not going to get any easier, for these are the CliffsNotes.

The World as Seen through a Glass of Ice Water

There are a billion reasons to look down
into a casket, but just one way to lie there dead,
which proves there isn't anything
you can think of that isn't here for the living,
who are each alive for a short time
in a very different way.
After she moves out, one tears up grass blades
to watch which way the wind blows.
Just over there, another buried
his favorite dog—and now look at that tree!
Would you like to model for me?
says the lousy painter
to every woman who walks within earshot.
Feeling a little dead?
Maybe you spend a weekend
faking a French accent,
maybe you buy an even more expensive stereo
and build a separate and self-sufficient world
inside the garage.
Something happens something happens something happens.
Repetition repetition repetition.
The saddest painting I ever saw
was on the carpet in my friend's hallway
where he tripped one night
carrying a gallon of red.
This was just before his divorce.
Just after he told me he was trapped
inside some idea of himself,
one he swore bore no relation
to what the rest of us had been seeing.
Nice shirt has always meant too many things.

Another Comeback Thought of Too Late

We were told to watch what we say,
though it soon became just another thought
we learned to live with, like the memory of a lost dog,
or the idea of moving to Memphis.
Anyplace warmer, or maybe a little more tarnished.
Here the sunlight surrenders too easily,
falling back into the tub, wrists slit.
And though we know it's not our fault,
at least not directly, we still search
for a more friendly face inside the medicine cabinet,
wondering whether this really is the best we could have done.
From beyond, dogs bray in their runs.
A plane rends the air with a scream,
like a muezzin calling the Azan.
Such is the nature of the cold:
it never stops catching us by surprise.
We've lived with it a long time,
and it's been a long time since
we've been able to say so,
though none want this to become the new way,
just another of the possible ways,
which, as they pass, will never get it right.
This is what has become of tradition.
Despite what the docent says,
those Japanese sculptures *were* meant to be touched.
And then, suddenly, here we are,
once again left stranded, deracinated, too self-aware,
prepared to shuffle back into the only normal
we know, scaring the pigeons beautiful
simply by walking past.

Fortune

The energy dissipates,
or whatever its distaff equivalent would be.
That said, geysers still spew from the catacombs.
When you shake their hand, always look them in the eye.
But how can I, you might ask, if they're selling
us subscriptions from Mumbai?
Suburban children often invent more ethnic childhoods,
and many succor heavenward, to be sure,
heaving in what's left of the mottled fields.
Beware of the darkness.
It's where the spies and their whiskers linger.

Limerence

The houses aren't speaking
to one another and neither is that
which lives within them, the stillness,
the already spoken for,
the speechless saying nothing
like a congregation to which everything
bears repeating, every one thing known
or even merely suspected to be: the snow,
which we knew was coming,
the snow that we never thought would be gone.
Like the moment we realized
we knew what one another was thinking,
which is how we awoke here,
chilling in our cadences, doubled in vain.
This is not what I wanted, thought one,
before the other placed a finger
on his lips. Before the sun withdrew
and threw another paternal darkness
over the earth. Before the house
groaned at a single, mournful pitch,
and a child, sure she was about
to be devoured alive, refused sleep.
Before the snow returned as the memory
of a thousand snows,
while in sleep, arms twitched
with the memories of a thousand shovelings,
each time convincing ourselves
that it is not suffering that keeps us here,
it is the chance for something more beautiful
for being closer to what we hope
we've been dying for all along.

For an Object to Float, It Must Displace Matter Equal to Its Weight

Today isn't over until I say it is,
so I won't ever again speak,
or so I mistakenly thought,
lying awake in the darkness
slowly swelling shut my eyes,
until they, too, blinked out.
Until on a remote mountaintop
I met the statue of the goddess
who awaits glory
with her marble hands stretched wide,
as if to show us that we'll never
get our arms around any of this,
beginning with our very abandonment here.
You can stand at the sink and punch
right through the suds
and still not find
the precious thing you left at the bottom.
When a dolphin dies,
it can take hours to rise to the surface,
which is where the hungry gulls
know to wait.

Fortune

It's not exactly as you would have had it: the rain
falls as freezing rain, the freezing rain falls as dying stars,
every neighbor stands in for some version
of yourself you long since became and discarded.
The gas station sells everything you need to escape,
which you buy in installments but never fully use,
having developed a set of responsibilities
binding you to everything you can touch.
In the way the cold or a sudden kiss from a stranger
might remind you that you still have a face
good for being more than a window you're forever looking through.

Fortune

Every image fosters an image. Each act enacts itself.
If the animals could speak,
we might be surprised to learn
that what they've been so desperate to tell us
is that many are in tremendous pain.
The farthest you can travel
from these kinds of thoughts is to
never father the very children who have them.
Good news: it may not be too late.
If you want to know whether or not your Mississippi works,
look down from above
to see if its leaves are moving.

Massage Farm

Out there it's Monday,
if you know where to look,
toward things merely parading
among the stalwart hopes
of a deliberate noon.
In here what things left
still simple and certain
perform their irrelevant maneuvers:
the disarrangement of Sunday's funnies,
this dough, which blushed and risen
has filed its own exposé
on the elastic and fumbled.
Was this what the forecast had called for?
Were those really angels,
or had the moon
grown yet another mustache?
The squirrels don't seem so caught up
in such cosmetics. For them it's all
another serenade to the reminding,
a bouquet of, well, what the hell's the difference?
Nobody's that good with names,
which like those antique dolls
were never meant to be played with,
certainly not like that, anyway.
Some are the currency of bored women,
some were pulled from ancient burial,
some both, and in this way every day
can be a kind of organ donor,
so how does that make you feel?
Eyes on your own paper!
Left alone upon the battlements,
the hours have again strung themselves
out before the grandstand

like circus elephants circled,
each girth more gaudily comparisoned,
every clown funnier by a parasol,
ludicrous shoes, plastic daisies
and the one who weeps
as he's forever unable to show himself out.

Civics Lesson

New to town, we didn't know how to speak the municipal language. But they kept us fed for as long as we could convincingly feign comprehension. We did this by smiling.

By day, some drove with their headlights on, the front license plates of the older cars perfectly askew. By night, they returned home, carefully hanging their clothes from wire sculptures bent to resemble shoulders. This went on for weeks.

The leaves changed color. Our camouflage proved useless. Eventually it got very cold.

When we slit the belly of a local snowman, we discovered a spine comprised entirely of the trickle of his own undoing. Their gods were gutless.

Everything was ceremony. Rubbish spilled from the park's centralized barrel. We watched them place crumpled bags and paper cups next to it, as if mere proximity were discarded enough.

But no one ever sat down in that park.

It was as if they couldn't stop moving.

Fortune

Your national anthem is whooping cough.
Lava is belched forth from the bottom
of an unexplored sea. At some point,
your idea of a good time became simply: the idea itself.
Somewhere the assholes are comparing cell phones.
Somewhere the insurgents are huddling in a cave.
Before wheeling the mannequin into the elevator,
the stylist unscrews its arms.
Some parts of us will always be extraneous.
Your neighbors are about to name the new school mascot
after an animal the neighborhood has never seen.

State Room

Whether or not you think you can,
this isn't some wet
paper bag you can tear
your way out of,
however ungorgeously or upheld
like a conviction to some light
or higher standard,
in the process pretending
to an aristocracy of elegantly feigned astonishments,
everyone thinking, *Why can't you
be more like your sister?*
This season they're saying
that red is the new black,
and so you can't help but dream
of everything in your life
you could have sent back to the kitchen.
It will count just as much then,
another instant in which you decide
your favorite song is whatever you think
you hear on the radio
just before you turn it on.
A real evening's kind of evening:
the utilities paid off,
the piano begging for moonlight,
and you, alone in a palace
that's always left on.

Upon Turning 35

What a difference a day can fail to make.
Surviving another moment measured in Mississippis,
another hour spent handcuffed to my watch.
Lately these are the only excuses I've had,
watching the governor's mansion glow evil with fake cheer,
the frost lower itself into the yard
as softly as every opera curtain I've ever dreamed.
Compared to 23, 35 is still more like 18
than 46, but what good does math do me now?
We weren't born in innocence,
we were born in much blood and suffering,
so every second counts.
I can barely get it all down.
There's a truck towing a truck
in front of a trailer delivering trailers,
my car basking in a split second
of silence beneath each overpass
before smashing back into the rain.
Once, in California, on my way to the sea,
I drove into a dense fog. I vowed then
I would someday make it back out.

Fortune

Every spill aspires to become a lake.
All decay aspires to the condition of Venice.
In 2008, you can contribute $15,500
to a tax-free retirement savings account.
The neighbors, who knows what the hell they're thinking.
In the splendid September sun, they go couch shopping.
They fall asleep at night praying to live
to see the day you cut down the juniper.
Their spines crave disassembly.
Pain reminds us that this moment is still here.
Happiness reminds us that it won't last forever.

The Saving of Daylight through Coordinated Adjustments in Time

There isn't any way to see it approaching
as indifferently as the very vacancy
we created, at a ludicrous speed,
cheating the sun, which it remains safest to see
by focusing off to one side.
Like the prayer where
at the beach we stand
and empty our pockets into the sea,
all we practice in sleep
has only to do with a later awakening.
The way a walk at night through the snow
is one's former silence
becoming the noise
that redefines the newer peace.
Spring trees still holding fall leaves.
Spring bird feeder holding nothing at all.
One hour swapped for a billion shards of light,
everything we've ever known mirrored there,
so that in convincing so many
to surrender at once it becomes a memory
never to be found,
because to make it we have slain
every part of ourselves
we cannot name.
It happened while we slept,
and most realize it now,
feeling somehow shorter,
or suddenly without exact change.
Already unable to recall
a seamlessness without manufacture,
here once again,
watching the sea write and then erase
our past upon the shore.

Skyscraper National Park

Fake trees never grow in the lobbies
not known for any bird or breeze.

Just outside the revolving doors,
smokers stand beneath tiny clouds
and plot their revenge.

Their children are at home,
ordering their feelings over the Internet,
charging them to the credit cards they were given
for keeping spring break domestic this year.

Secretly beneath skirts, secretaries' thongs
slice through the Minneapolis night.

Refrigerated trucks shuttle what's left
of cattle carcasses into the industrial plant.

Above the national forest of television antennae,
unmanned spy drones migrate south,
looking for someplace to nest.

Like birds, they invented flying
to find something new to eat.

Fortune

Water always can be found
in close proximity to water.
Or so you discover while
snorkeling in your own lagoon.
You have to lose her
to truly miss her. Yet you also have to miss her
to truly appreciate how lucky you are
that she's never left.
There is very little you can do now.
Dreams, like wayward whales, echolocate in the deep.
On this planet, only humans
can remove their clothes without fear.

Fortune

Swimming pools are painted blue
to let you know it's okay to jump.
It must be when we're not looking
that the empty porch chairs know to circle.
You'll know you have a beaver problem
when your Mississippi stops.
But you may never know there are wasps
nesting in your soffits.
In the flood-ravaged city, a man fashions a raft
out of the few belongings he has left
and is unwilling to die without.
On the old maps, beyond the edges of what was known to be,
they drew monsters.

Beached

As long as what will destroy us
is the uneasy beauty that, for our lives,
we'll never understand.
As long as we long for the old stories
and even the grace
with which we're sure we once told them,
neither forgotten, nor forgiven,
beach-house hammocks sighing in the breezeway,
window fans whispering with secrecy
to the shirts shifting in the closet, as if to say,
Isn't it time you did something
about this part of yourself you keep hidden?
One answer has been to ignore the question,
another to take a lifetime in response,
because for every moment it's the memory
of how her shoulders felt in your hands,
there's another when it's the mere idea
they held them at all,
as this part of the world turns
from the sun and the darkness falls
along the shore with pointless omen,
as the first of the bathers
recognize the beginnings of their good-byes,
the tinny shouts of pleasure
already dissolving into a namelessness
our hearts cannot hold.
The reasons aren't all that urgent
and the days will have none of it,
another evening not quite reflecting its larger age,
another past that does us no good
because it has no future.
It's simply a place where people refused
to smile for a portrait.

A place full of funny bicycles,
a handful of spiders, which are always
filling in the corners. Below: lovers,
desperate for darkness, fumble for the switch,
tangling themselves in postures of pleasure
they swear they invented,
as if to fend off the realization
they're trapped in the same cycle of desire,
here beneath a sky of clouds
and everything that isn't clouds,
a bay of sailboats reflecting perfect sailboats,
a beloved undressing herself right back into smoke,
right back into the world's own wishful thinking.

3

Push

Shouldn't it be different this time,
or shouldn't there be another reason why,
the same woman applying blush in the bus
in which the day's paper is always there in the seat for you?
It's even harder to survive the routine
when it becomes the last thing that's holding you together.
Long after you leave, the soap still dissolves
in the dish from the memory of your hand.
In your hand, lunch in a plastic bag.
Later, in the rain, a bike seat wrapped in the one thing left of it.
In the descending darkness, a welder
electrocutes the condominium skeleton.
He thinks of the woman in the circus there to prove
herself most beautiful by riding the horse backwards.
They call it "falling" asleep
because discovering you have nothing to hold onto
is how it always begins.
They'll know I was a dreamer
when they see what little is left of my bones.

Vertical Hold

When in even our recent histories
we ask ourselves how it is we have arrived
here where the snow
goes on like this forever
beneath a series of skies that can't,
plain glass stained only by what we see
through it, the seeing stopped only
by the reflections staring back.
These storms are never as beautiful
as their afterwards are,
an echo always over there,
a car wash hunched over in the night,
a jacket hung from the hook
that proves some part of us has already given up.
The stars gaze back and name
the patterns we form, too.
One for footprints in the snow,
another for skyscraper warning beacons
flashing through the cloud deck,
or the way that woman's hair
moves back from her face
as the train approaches,
in the same way a windsock
is forever alerting us
to just one of the things we're up against,
like amnesia, or whatever word
is the opposite of amnesia, we forget.
Today is for recycling, tomorrow trash.
A hawk is in our cloud.
A wind blows a cloud in our sky above home.
A dull, indefatigable light.
Alone, the snow is turning to water.
Together, that water will make the sea.

Depth Charged

If form should follow function,
what should follow form?
Now days, even salads come with meat.
The comedian looks out into the dark
and waits for laughter.
The deep-sea explorer looks out into the dark
and just waits.
Even ten miles beneath the surface,
you're still the one person
you can never say good-bye to.
But you can discover new species of jellyfish—
slowly, as it means first inventing
new kinds of submarines.
Just like a jellyfish, you think you're a bad ass,
yet you're both comprised almost entirely of water and a T-shirt.
There are insurgents who even now
are readying their fuses.
There's a billionaire
circling the planet in a nylon balloon.
For more than half of the journey
there's nothing to see but ocean,
but you don't need to spend a week
in a basket to learn that.
Just buy a paper from the mouth
of one of those cheap robots chained
to a No Parking sign.
It will tell you that most everything
is simply water and space,
even cancer. *We've entered the knowledge economy,*
says the president in today's edition.
A boy is taught to turn himself into a bomb.
A taxi later explodes in Ramallah.
This morning, poetry seems impossible.

There's a sinister glow to these highway lights.
Lilacs, from white to purple, fade late here in May,
schools of electric minnows blink red in the deep.
And then sleep enters our homes,
always at the very moment
we float away and leave them.

Fortune

The shopping mall's surface lot spreads out
its all-u-can-eat buffet of convenient parking.
No nation's children will inherit more asphalt.
Mattresses sleep in their discount warehouses.
Executives can't,
worrying they're running out of places
to underpay people to serve overpriced coffee.
The neighbors are eavesdropping,
if only on the faint hiss of your shower.
A man unwraps his morning paper
and hopes for the best.
Truly desperate acts are rarely witnessed,
except by truly desperate men.

Fortune

Some love thunder, others bored after the flash,
there's silence, then silence, then several more tons
of ice fracture from the continental shelf.
Maybe these very thoughts literally *are* God,
and we're not so much having them, as God is having us.
I'm the decider, and I decide what's best.
The department store lights flick out,
and the mannequins vanish onto the dark side of zero.
Thunder. Flash.
Your neighbors have neighbors who suspect their neighbors.

61 Titles Unpoemed

1. Colonial Voice-over
2. When That I Had Bus-Stop Patience
3. Go Deep
4. A New Category of Response to Beautiful Women
5. I Am the Stinger, I Am the Stung
6. The 90-Percent-Solution Solution
7. Ode to Emancipated Minors
8. Real Falling
9. *From* Book XVI: The Lingerie Wars
10. Why Me Poet
11. Mother's Little Helper
12. Administered Topically
13. Red Buttons
14. I Being the One
15. Negative Culpability
16. Baggage Claim
17. The Experience of an Old World Shave
18. To Anastasio Valdez and His Aching Tummy
19. Start Seeing Motorcycles
20. Boyhood Wallpaper
21. Don't Shake It (Monk Rock)
22. The Wrong Shoes Will Always Give You Away
23. The Secret Life of Puppets
24. Bar Code
25. Music for Lacing One's Tennies
26. Moo Goo Gai Pan
27. Place No Object Here
28. Licensed to Beg
29. When Man Discovered He Could Invisibly Deliver Moving Pictures with Sound
30. Breathe through Your Mouth
31. Can I Get a Witness?
32. {"Three beers strong, we braved those seen in passing"}

From Beyond the Arc

Where have we been for so long
that leaves us with the suspicion
we've gone nowhere at all?
Watch running fast, clock slow,
screaming at the drive-time radio.
Another day here awakening
to the usual light,
staring out of the two holes in a standard head,
mumbling in praise while scavenging
for forgiveness, leaning into
one another or watching her watch you watch her
unbutton her dress to stave off
the loneliness of a brand new day
in the same old world.
In the middle of the sea,
a captain prays to his map
as his ship slips
slowly beneath the surface,
and not a single cry is heard.
It's that easy to be erased.
So stand up. So state your name.
As if you're communicating
with the world at the speed of smoke signal.
To fix your heart,
first they saw you open,
then they pack your chest
entirely in ice.

Peripeteia

Whatever you say, but not before
establishing the questions
for which the answer has always been no:
a third bottle, never telling her,
kissing back, leaving or being left.
The sign says *No Smoking,*
yet here we sit, slowly turning into vapor.
In the kitchen, just that bouquet of knives.
In the mattress, the lasting impression,
over the years, we all leave behind.
Like the memory of every snow angel
that has ever asked you to forget
that angels never lie down.
And the questions for which the answer
was always yes. And the reflection
returned from the headlights: those eyes,
just before you turned to go.
But we're not thinking these thoughts,
the chemicals in our brains are.
Now try saving someone's life.

Fortune

Your good fortune for today:
Brooke's Bitchin' Morning Special,
the El Diablo Breakfast Sandwich and a pancake, $5.95.
Served just before the city spreads itself before you
as your greatest single possession.
Soon you will come across an empty stroller
abandoned in the heat.
You will realize that your wish
was granted long ago, and it is unclear
what purpose it will possibly serve now.

Happiness

What say we say
something ridiculous without
seeming resigned to it, just weightless
and alive and chasing after
as little gravity as possible here.

Fish dream of escaping
the county reservoir.

They're like every version
of yourself waiting to be retrieved
from the dry cleaner,
passing the time
just spinning around and around.

We all fear
happiness because it's always
about to end,
and so, in itself, an ending.

It was the feel of a decaying wooden
dock that first taught you
what it meant
to have feet.

Reaching down into the water,
you shook chains
lashed to old tires,
and the fish vanished.

In the underwater moonlight,
the chains fell silent,
and you vanished.

Same Light, Different Lightning

Even standing at the gate,
I could not pronounce the name of the ancient palace.

I had traveled unrecognized,
though one there would soon call me father.

I visited two palaces,
each built to insure the other from fire,

just as you have been given two names,
each there to protect the other.

Each name is a prayer for you.

When I first dreamed of you, I dreamed
a queen had entrusted me with your life.

When I dreamed of you a second time,
I awoke back inside the first,
and this is how I learned the way home.

When I say your names, I say the prayers.
I can't wait for you to tell me your side of the story.

Say your names and become many,
for you are the lovely many.

Say your names and become queen.
You may now choose your palace.

Fortune

The rich wife adjusts her marriage's Super Bowl ring
and rises from the bath, reliving the horror of her own birth.
The rich husband begins another surgery by leaving
his signature incision in the abdomen of an anaesthetized patient.
The police cruiser idles in the alley like a shark in a dying coral reef.
There's a street beneath this street, a city beneath this city,
inhabited entirely by empty tunnels
built for trains that never arrived.
We fold our laundry into shapes that help it to remember us.
It takes just one blood test to know you,
so you have to be careful where you bleed.

Fortune

Sometimes, at night, you walk past
the neighbors' windows, hoping to catch just a glimpse.
Sometimes you climb back into your PJs and try to start the day again.
The stuntman, set ablaze, stumbles across the set.
The splinters of destruction fall from the mannequin's spine.
A thousand bouquets of gas-station roses
are left to die upon the graves of a thousand war veterans.
Don't step in that puddle.
You never know who that might have been.

Summer Offensive

Like a supposed come-on
translated into yet another language
you'll never understand,
danger is born in beauty
and descent, an old bike traveling
an even older hill,
a streetlight thrown
through a row of tequila shots
lined up and waiting at the bar.
The ferns swell in diffuse light.
Indistinct from their own shadows,
the shadows yawn into night.
A woman strays from her recipe.
The food knots in the throat.
A child closes his eyes
and slowly gives in, wetting the bed.
The captain throws the engines into reverse.
Discount tires, groceries browsed
in warehouses, trousers with a medium break.
In the middle of an empty freezer in June,
a snowball waits.

No Wake

In the Museum of Radiant Heat, two performance artists fight over adjustments to the thermostat in a jejune commentary on the persistence of relativity in an increasingly technological world. On the top floor of an office building in Cape Canaveral, a man cleans the hallway with a vacuum cleaner strapped to his back, because it's the closest he can get to being an astronaut. In a windowless classroom at the University of Suspicious Sweaters, a professor tells his students he is going to explain it all carefully in a way that makes sense, yet will sound completely made up. A woman, trying to tell her husband that she has planned her own death, plants daffodils in his briefcase. Carrying our ghosts, motorcycles pass in the night. Two lovers walk along the river and agree that it's over, the river of course just a metaphor for the misunderstandings that drift between them, though the current is quite real. The woman closes the briefcase. A motorcycle backfires. The professor looks at his class and says nothing. The wife looks at her husband, and the husband looks at his wife, and a small child says, *Fine, you're both right.*

In the Middle of Every Zero Is a Center That Will Not Hold

At first, the darkness will feel like a mistake,
but it will not be a mistake,
for unlike the world, oblivion is perfect.
The x-rays show nothing.
The divers never have to surface.
And at a limitless, late hour,
an old man wakes
only to roll over and fall asleep again.
It's an abandoned town that has no memory of being a town,
and the river that feeds it
ran dry long before you were born.
But the ruthless no longer go unpunished,
and your leader can't mangle the mother tongue.
The young men and women he sentenced to infinity there
lay down their rifles and head for the hills
in a gesture that has no moment to hold it,
and if you could make just one prediction,
there would be only one prediction to make,
and you'd always be right.
Good-bye, sweet guesswork.
Poems, a critic recently announced,
need to go back to being about things.
About from the Old English *abutan,*
meaning *on the outside.*
Everyone likes having a ghost to worship,
another side to suspect,
people who we know will never need us.
In the middle, whatever's multiplied is still null.
The silence that precedes the beginning,
the different one that follows the end.
Before the lightning strikes the pine straw,

or the ball washes up on the beach.
Before the ball. Before even the beach.
But maybe after you finish washing your bowl.
After just a little running water.

The Portable Whitman

Everywhere. And waiting for you.
And suddenly it's been a full day since
anyone last gave up or allowed
another poem to end with light, and
in that you can find your own beginnings.
Entire embassies of listening,
the cumulative two years
anyone will spend rummaging through closets.
The race is on and always has been.
A tree middles the meadow,
yet another excuse for the disinclination
of most scenes to resolve themselves.
A baseboard chill sweeping the leg,
every pane of glass that can be cleared
with a palm that once hushed a young boy's mouth.
Persuasion is an art that you must first
perform quietly for yourself.

Fortune

Don't give up on this just yet. The insomniacs are fighting
over the blankets. They are under the impression
that their religion-versus-science conflict is new,
a result of their own cleverness, perhaps?
But you've suffered far longer atop your sandals
amid this pilgrimage from inn to unassuming inn,
the sound of last night's rain still enduring its downspout.
It is here that you will surrender your affectations.
It is here, gnats clinging to the screen,
that you can finally sleep.

Cash 'n' Carry Bouquet

He's trying to put the future behind him, navigating the oldest avenues on his way to the museum. Beneath the grotesques of passing clouds, bungalows doze low in the sun. Thoughts vibrate at a pitch he hadn't sensed before—and if he knows just one thing, it's that he wants no one's charity.

Inside, the air is cool, like a palace, a place it becomes appropriate to think European things, which arrive at the speed of the absence of light. Gliding through the galleries, through their bleached rooms and statuary, he can't help but wonder, does any of this really solve anyone's problems?

By the time he leaves, the letter will have been left in the mailbox, this much is known. Though he's pretty sure he knows exactly how the baby will feel before he finally has her in his arms.

Civil Twilight

I saw a stranger ride past on an even stranger bicycle,
one that had spent too many years in this world's greenhouse,
another occurrence brief enough
to be constructed of its own relief,
the suburbs, and then, at last, the last suburbs,
for now anyway, indeterminacy never announcing its fluctuations,
one last summer saw whining late into the solstice
of work and the mothers of this work,
the few jewels they have to wear around their necks
and the sounds of their children
as they slowly outgrow their own bathtubs.
The last of the sun and a sudden deference to same such.
Arms at your sides, you'll be asked for nothing.
I saw a stranger pause after dragging from the strange cigarette,
and she held there inside her breath, inside of herself,
all of the available data and contradictions of the moment,
curating her own profusion like all of those people
in all of those airports just waiting there.
Who doesn't suspect they would never be friends
with themselves if they weren't already forced *to be* themselves?
Even now your slippers sit by the bedside.
The bed sits along the seaside.
The sea throws itself against the rocks,
and the rocks slowly give in,
and already your new map has it wrong.
It's all water under the bridge,
bridge under the unassailable starlight,
everything staring back into the business end of this moon's business,
the pain of the double-paned
glass of the lifestyle merchants, their showrooms
full of things that are themselves lovely imitations
of older and even lovelier things,
lost steamer trunks, genuine denim,

a trolley that used to be a trolley, a trolley that's now a bus,
every fleeting thought of the famous and the dead
and everything we're supposed to remember they said.
The horror and beauty of the elaborately cruel reality
left once the pleasant lies are gone.
The sound of the millionairess ringing her servant's bell one final time.
From the window of a descending eastbound flight,
pools shimmer in the last light of
the city after you've left the city, now back,
the sylvan parks, the shoreline
and its negative sediment budget.
Confusion and ecstasy: there's not much else to go on here.
An extension cord is plugged into an extension cord
is plugged into an extension cord.
Characters greet one another in time,
or fret about it, and how devoted it is to its own passing.
The ice falls through the darkness
into the motel dispenser's tiny bucket
and then, finally, there's another dose of atmospheric feedback
to stylishly articulate our brightly modern selves
withstanding our darkly adolescent woes.
What else might say it?
Night after night now, a little glass of wine with dinner.
To prove the new bridge was sturdy,
the government sent elephants across first,
yet another parade that seemed to read our minds.

Acknowledgments

I'm grateful to the editors of the following journals for first publishing these poems: *Columbia Poetry Review; Conduit; Forklift, Ohio; Gulf Coast; H_NGM_N; Incliner; jubilat; The Laurel Review; LIT; Luna; The Modern Review; New Ohio Review; Octopus; Pool; Post Road;* and *Third Coast.*

A grant from the Jerome Foundation and the Loft helped to make this book possible.

Thank you to my family and to the many friends who have supported me during the writing of these poems, including Dean Young, Steve Healey, Derik Newman, The Gooch, Amanda Nadelberg, Chris Fischbach, and Paula Cisewski.

I would especially like to thank Jeff Shotts, Katie Dublinski, and everyone at Graywolf HQ, as well as Matt Hart and William D. Waltz for their ideas and inspiration.

Eternal embrace: Kathy.

Dobby Gibson's previous collection of poetry,
Polar, won the Beatrice Hawley Award.
He lives in Minneapolis.

The text of this book has been set in Adobe Garamond Pro, drawn by Robert Slimbach and based on type cut by Claude Garamond in the sixteenth century. This book was designed by Ann Sudmeier. Composition by BookMobile Design and Publishing Services, Minneapolis, Minnesota. Manufactured by Versa Press on acid-free paper.